Hydration

An Arizona Poetry Collection

Volume 1, Autumn 2024

Editor's Note
Cierra C. Crea, Surprise

Thank you so much for buying PopTab Press's inaugural issue of *Hydration*. I've titled this project after the thing we all need most in this Arizona desert. Like water, poetry is what gives many of us the will to keep going when everything feels so painfully dry here. This first volume was made to uplift the voices of local poets, but it may grow in scope as time goes on. You will see work from many of the people who performed on stages in 2024 at events like Fruity Poetry Night, Ghost Poetry Show, PHX Poetry Slam by B-Jam, and many more. This is a first publication for many of them.

I'm immensely proud and grateful to be able to create this platform, and will continue to do so as long as I have the capacity. I deeply appreciate you, dear reader, and anyone else who helped me make this project a reality.

Enjoy!

CONTENTS

Kaden Presley, Gilbert

The Five Seasons of the Sonoran Desert in Haiku

Jackson Ercil Evans, Scottsdale

Winter Solstice
Winter in my tea
Morning stars shine white and cold
The world is and is

Spring
Pink cactus flowers
Bloom as wide as the desert
How rich the dry air!

First Summer
Birds sing of summer
A mosquito adds its voice
Now a full choir

Monsoon Season
The next day
And the rain has left footprints
In the sand

Autumn
Autumn night, full moon
Exhausted of nostalgia
But what can I do?

Oasis

Touch Me Tender
Nye Cox, Chandler

I can feel the reverence
When you ask is this okay
Before dancing your fingers across
The vulnerable parts of my lower back
And even in this moment
I'm trying to give yes the weight that it needs

Because what I mean is
I have learned how to love myself well
Yet some healing I can't do on my own
Love was grown and woven into me in the womb
But I was born without knowing a safe place
To put my trust

What I mean is
I have known many touches
That have drained the life from me
Because I had love to give
And my body
Is still learning how not to flinch
When something soft reaches towards me

What I mean is
I don't always know
How to let in the things that I desire
To let them reach the things that are dead in me
To remember to breathe when they do
To let the softness
Soften me too

What I mean is
Yes
Please
Touch me

First Green
Catherine Sullivan, Phoenix

The first green of spring mattered so much to you
so even after it all
I always make a note of it
just to think that somewhere
you're still smiling.

In a different world
that means something.
In a different world
I run into you at the bookstore,
maybe tomorrow, maybe in two years,
and things are different.
We get to talking, we get to coffee,
we slowly work our way back into each other's lives.
And yes, it'll never be the same,
but in a different world, I could find my way back to your side.

But look around.
I have a life now
and I'm deciding to keep it.
I'm moving.
Michigan won't be home anymore.
You won't be home anymore.
There won't be a bookstore reunion.

Look around.
It's the middle of the desert.
There is no first green of spring here.

Lazy Sunday
Leah Serrano, Tucson

Sunshine streams in
Skin on skin
Sweat streaked sheets
Tangle of limbs
Open and whole
Hungry and full
Languid lovers

You tell me you love me, say
I don't have to say it back
If I don't want to
But how can I explain?
My dear, I have never really loved anyone
But you

i want(ed) to matter

Kivy Brown, Gilbert

there is something so profound about the way my own words sit on my tongue, pressing back into my throat and threatening to gag me out from the source. garbled gibberish. is that what you hear when i speak? this isn't a metaphor, i'm choking the idea of you. trying to swallow it down. you were somebody completely different a year ago and i don't recognize your face

anymore. your name has no meaning in the pits of my belly. yet, after all this time, it still holds the weight of the world. ~~my love,~~ you are crushing me down. tell me if i did something wrong. let me know i meant something to you. is our sunburn starting to peel from me? ~~stop moving on without me.~~ no amount of anesthesia could help me through this extraction of you. ~~my~~ aloe vera, promise me i will make it through this with less scarring than before. ~~don't let this romanticization take me down without you.~~

Sapphic
Fera Florescence, Tempe

Sapphic is such a soft word, and I am sick of the lesbians calling our love such a soft word;
Their poetry mocks what you have left me with.

I wish I could call you the plush sand along the rolling beach shores,
But you are the seashell stabbing my naked feet, so beautifully you attack,
Keeping me on my toes, cracking apart when I'm too close.

I wish I could symbolize your skin to the bedsheets we laid in,
But you are the blood stain that just won't come out, no kindness in this rotted, cotton wash,
Soaking into my clothes, wearing into my woes.

No, I cannot call you my oasis in this wasteland
As you are a creosote unbinding with the rain,
Exhaling ozone, breaking down in the strangest of occasions,

You fragile leaf, you sensitive thing.

And it's probably as simple of a conclusion that this partnership was not meant to be.
My restless sun rays of ashamed anxious flames
Thawed away the patience encasing your anger;
That's definitely on me.

But I really hate the way they talk about a love we could never share.

Tamed and Restrained
Audrey Sher-Walton, Tucson

Been tamed and restrained for so long
You unleash my wild streak

I'm not those things you say I am
Daring, crafty-no not me.

But something about you
leads me to this aberrant behavior
my sensuality, femininity set free

A part of me is cordoned off-open only to you
A piece of me that no one else can infiltrate
A sliver only recently unearthed

I keep you sequestered from the rest of the world; my own private caprice

I send you the core of me, the hidden me, unwrapped
You drink me in, devour me
And then return for more

Always you appear-
A silent voice rippling inside my head
The soft breeze that moves my curls against my shoulders

Whispers, the hint of your touch
pierces

And you
you've never even inhaled
my perfume

Fragments (Haiku)
Rynnie Kate, Chandler

You, me, architects
When we were building something
I thought was holy

Featured Poet:

Cristina (Cree) Port

Cristina or Cree Port, (she/her) is a Minnesota native turned Phoenix transplant. She has a BS in biological sciences from Arizona State University, is a musician and music teacher specializing in multiple instruments, a proud pet owner, a person who orders the same coffee drink every time, and a writer/poet. She is a winner of the 2024 Copper Courier poetry submission competition with her poem, "I'm Not in Love, but I Wanted to Pretend I was so I Wrote This." A 3rd place winner in the Phoenix Ghost Poetry Slam, and a feature poet at the August 2024 Fruity Poetry open-mic night hosted at the Phoenix Art Museum. If she's not writing or playing an instrument, she loves to dance, eat the Trader Joe's sweetened dried orange slices, roller-blade, play hockey, and take public transit to new places just for fun.

I'm not in love, but I wanted to pretend I was so I wrote this.

So I drop everything to race and tag her through a breezy field on a sunny day tripping
on tall weeds and flowers from sprinting too fast.
Giggling and heaving in air.

Our silhouette's held by the grass,
painting hearts on each other with dandelions and holding hands to lips to whistle for
loons but end up getting dizzy breathing out air and laughing even harder.

And when she looks at me,

with that look.

The kind that causes my brain to glitch like a 2000's computer, nonverbal dial tone,

That look,

makes me want her

to look at me like that forever.

Her hands pulling me towards her face,
asking if I'm still in there,
asking for me to be closer,
needing to be closer.
"One more time." But maybe say that a thousand billion times.

But that's just it:

It's getting into the car at 1 am trying each and every McDonald's to find the ice cream
machine that works.

It's how I'll hold her thigh while she drives and I get to hear
her laugh that sounds like Pantone's 2023 color of the year "Viva Magenta" suspended in
an IV bag being sucked into my dry veins and winding its way through my body to
bloom like bougainvillea that's been trimmed just right.

Sitting on the front porch in rocking chairs with our coffee, slightly cold and damp, as the
rain starts to slap the roof, the sky's comments grumbling to spook her into my lap,

hands out to catch the water rolling off our skin like diamonds falling into a pile I'll throw
into the sky to make constellations

and name them after the things she likes so she won't be alone when she gets lost.

And she'll lasso and I'll wrangle the moon into our living room corral,
so that we can ebb and flow, together.
Crossing my heart, staining my sheets, plunging feet first into the Pacific ocean knowing
our bodies will always be warmer tangled together.

Because it's about (un)buckling the seat belt and saying,
"Hold on, I'm coming with you."

For one more game of tag and a dandelion tattoo.
For one more fruitless round of finding the ice cream machine that works.
For one more coffee and rocking in tandem when it rains.
For one more kiss in the drive-through because we gave up on McDonald's and Taco Bell
was the last thing open.

For one more time,
but really a thousand billion times,
plus one,

one more time.

If Jesus Was A Modern Catholic Millennial

If Jesus was a modern Catholic millennial, he would wear real Birkenstocks he bought for full price before he went on his abrupt spiritual journey through Germany that he paid for with his parents credit card he stole when they took him to lunch three weeks ago.

He would practice opening his third eye on the way to Trader Joe's to get some vegan hummus and probably avoid eye contact with people when he doesn't buy beyond meat because he doesn't want to be fake but also can't quite give up real blood.

He probably tells his friends that doing coke at a rave is a direct line to God, (or wait was that actually just a k- hole?) and that in order to lead a spiritual life you had to help yourself first before others so he ignores the people next door starving since he's got an entire freezer filled with emotional support drugs with enough space for one Torino's pizza roll bag his mom paid for.

If Jesus was a modern Catholic millennial, he probably wouldn't even be Catholic but rather take certain parts of religions he didn't quite understand, warping them into a huge clusterfuck of symbols like trinkets of chakras, buddhas, jade dragons, burning white sage, repeatedly playing Sufjan Stevens Carrie and Lowell vinyl, using tea tree oil as deodorant,

Basically if he was a coffee shop barista, he'd be an asshole.

He'd tell everyone his poetry was the gospel but really he stole quotes from Rupi Kaur and even though its it's not explicitly mentioned in the King James Bible next to the Book of Mormon in his Vegas hotel split with the 12 boys, he definitely wouldn't be a virgin and he'd claim he would never love again after cheating on his girlfriend Mary Magdalene but why commit when you've got the holy trinity!

Tinder, bumble, and Hinge plus. (He paid for it)

And if Jesus was a modern catholic millennial he'd most likely be a straight white man, but if he was queer, he wouldn't date bisexual or trans people or
BIPOC people but it's okay because he's still a member of the LGBTQIA+ group so he's not a terf or racist or sexist since he's gay so how could he perpetuate hate in his own community. Not slay.

And Jesus may say he's not an "all lives matter" kinda guy, but his dad's a cop so he also refuses to say all cops are bastards. He'd also be a Zionist. Probably a congressman when he decides to cut his hair.

See, the guy we know named Jesus won't ever be able to find himself by meditating in the vortexes of Sedona. He's never going to own up to being the creepy guy in the back of a yoga class because he'd say, "if you're uncomfortable don't wear leggings then."

And with his white person dreads, smelly balls, and painted nails, Jesus will avoid the wood splinters of vulnerability and metal spikes of accountability because,

If Jesus was a modern catholic millennial, he'd say,

"that's just who I am, for better or for worse, I treat everybody this way."

Dear Natalie,

Do you remember how we had boyfriends?

Because I still remember your perfume radiating onto the cards when we played slap jack while our boyfriends would kiss.

I can still remember when I told you I loved you.
And we could be in love,
But we couldn't be in love.

We couldn't kiss goodbye.

We couldn't sit in the one singular coffee shop with arms draped over each other's knees.

We couldn't post photos or hold hands.

So we gambled.

Our secrets shaken up in the backseats of our parents' cars on the backroad with the engine still running and foggy windows, hoping the cops wouldn't find us asking why two girls had no clothes on after prom.

"Oh we were just changing!"

We rolled the dice.

My first kiss with a woman was with a girl in my health class when I was 16 and she told me she lit her ex-girlfriend's mom's car on fire. Another girl had an ex boyfriend who sent me a letter, numbered 1-27 of the things she liked, and 28 was the death threat. It was terrifying but,

Who could I tell?

That when they wrote FAGGOT on the back of my car in the winter dirt,

Who could tell?

And the embarrassing part was that I couldn't just wipe the words off with one hand, I used my coat sleeves to wipe the whole back trunk. I wasn't able to wipe my tears.

Because I couldn't tell.

All I knew was that someone caught my bluff and I was losing, I needed more deception
to throw on the table so I played penny slots with the boys I dated and never slept with. I
know I wasn't alone, but

that's the danger of losing a bet.

Losers were put in the psych ward for being "unwell". The ward had a blessed crucifix
frozen in the foundation of the hospital, watching our minds be sealed in concrete molds
made from prozac and vicodin dyed blue for boys and pink for girls to make purple
when crushed together.
That "Stick it" and "She's the Man" were not about sporty queer women coming out of ice
baths, but rather, really, really, really, really, really, REALLY, close friends.

So, if we were sent there, they gave you a rosary to wrap around your neck and a sturdy
beam built by your own mutilated spirit and a chair placed under your feet by your
school friends who hoped you'd just die anyways because god didn't build a table big
enough for people like us to sit at.

Jesus wouldn't save you when you slipped off the stool.

That's how your debt is forgiven. Go in Peace.

So, I held my rosary in my hand,
And I taught Sunday school.
Leviticus 18:22 "Thou shalt not lie with mankind as with womankind; it is an
abomination."
I taught Paul's Letters, 1 Corinthians 6:9 - nice.
"We hate the gays"
I taught people that the word of their god was true.
So I lied,
religiously.

And if I was gonna sin, I was going double or nothing, so I called my parents to extend
my curfews to spend a few more hours with you Natalie. We made up "school projects" to
see each other on weekends. Smiling at each other in class, holding hands under the
desks during movies. Having snowball fights that ended in our red faces with chapped
lips smushed together. That driving in the car and being able to grab thighs and blow
bubbles out the windows and chase the lightning going 100 miles an hour on boring
straight roads were the moments we got to be ourselves.

The moments we got to be in love.

Because to be queer, means you have lied.
Because to be queer, (as of now) means you have to.
Because our quiet refusal to not be ourselves in truth

outweighed the lies we squeezed behind.
I kept my truth in a metal poker case with love notes I was given from the girls I loved. I bought used queer books online, and stacked them with the pages facing out and a harry potter book on top.
(And I think the moldy walls should've gone harder!)

I got an android to keep my parents from tracking me and reading my texts.
and yes I did sacrifice my blue texts to be gay!

We used real ropes anchored to giant trees to swing off the river bluffs into warm water with our really really really really really close friends we were romantically dating and having sex with.

We knew that in the end, if we made it out, pockets lined with loaded dice and magic trick cards, it would be worth it.

Because we were afraid

and yet,

we weren't afraid to try.

Drought

I Wish He Could Have Seen the Thunderstorm
Renee Bryant, Phoenix

I wish he could see
The lighting in the distance
From my airplane window
As I fly to Dallas Texas
To catch another flight
To Tyler international
To attend his funeral.

We were only ever
on an airplane together
A handful of times--
Once, on our honeymoon,
Twice back home for Christmas,
And that was all.

I always got the window seat-
And when I'd point at something
out the window
and say, "Look!"
His reply was like clockwork:
"Aw, cool."
And he'd amuse himself for one second
And me for four seconds longer,
Before turning back to his center seat,
Knees at a harsh 45,
To keep his 6'6 body from bothering anybody
But himself.

The last time I saw him before his deathbed
Was the day I stormed out of the bank.
I had clipped back the rage on my tongue
And said it with my body instead:
"Congratufuckinglations.
I see you aren't wearing your wedding ring.
Did you lose hers too?"

Four years later I'm holding his hand
In grandma Linda's new house,
A house she thought she'd never

Have to bury another
Son or husband in,
But now in horror
Watches as her grandson's ghost
Settles in
to the newly arranged guest room.

I held his hand for about three hours that night
And watched him eat one of his last meals
(Certainly the last piece
of Barro's pepperoni pizza dipped in ranch).

There was nothing much I said
Because I said it with my body instead
"I'm doing amazing-
You can be at peace knowing you did the right thing
For both of us
Thank you for being uniquely you"

On a lighter note,
he asked me if I was seeing anyone
I said Yes to keep things simple
And he said, like clockwork
"Aw, cool"
He read my body
Like the notes
we used to pass in high school
And he said with a smirk
"You're probably more
Experienced than even me now"

With not a hint of jealousy,
Because you can't be jealous
of someone you wanted to lose.
I beamed with pride and laughed
"Much more."

His sunken banana yellow skin
Was like a sunken suit of a man I once knew,
As if to say "There are six years here that are all brand new"
Six unknown years of sunsets, sex, backyards and breakfast,
But his eyes took me straight back to the past
and my hand relaxed.

We were finally separate.

A glass wall between us
Hands pressing and eye contact burning
We both knew it was our final goodbye.

Nothing but love when I saw him for the very last time
But I still wished he could have seen the thunderstorm.
He would have thought it was cool.

Silk and Steel
H. D. Dean, Phoenix

There is a value in vulnerability.
No one taught me, how could I know?
In a house where words were weapons
Children like me weren't raised but forged in fire.
Placed on an anvil and struck. Again. Again. Again.
Now all that's left is cold, warped steel.
You can still see the embers hidden in my brown eyes.
Never looking for violence but always ready
Sleeping with a sword at my side.
And I'm so fucking jealous.
Of girls made of chiffon and blue velvet
Whose hearts and minds have an open door policy.
People who are soft, not sharp and heavy like me.
People who can tell the difference between fireworks and gunshots
People who got the silver spoon and not the fucking hammer.
Everyone adores you, how could they not?
You scare me, I want to be you.
I want you to cut deep between rib and sternum
Crack ivory bones to hunt for precious emeralds.
Slice me open, see if I bleed raw garnets and rubies.
Who knows, maybe you'd find a pink pearl.
Nestled right between my liver and my lungs.
What if surgery can help me learn to trust like you?
What if my insides are smoother than I expected?

Presence of Absence (Letter to Sarah)
Rachel G., Tempe

Dear Sarah
I wish there was a word for me to describe
How your physical absence manifests itself in my life
Your body is no longer here as it was
That much I understand
It only exists as a pile of ashes where your columbarium now stands
And yet...I almost feel like...
If I were to reach far enough
Stretch my arms out wide
That maybe
Just maybe
I would be able to hug you again
Hold your hand one more time
Does that make me insane?
Crazy?
Out of my mind?
My brain
Can't take
These reminders of my pain
This weight
I will always carry
This guilt that I can't shake
Your absence is so present in my life
But YOU are always a little too far away
I feel the need to say
I'm sorry
I feel like I did you wrong
There must have been some reason you wanted to leave
Was it my fault?
Why did you not open up to me?
Was I not a good big sister?
Were we just never as close as I thought we were?
There's this funny thing about grief, right?
It goes round and around in my mind
Torturing my consciousness
With thoughts of
What could've been
Like every action another person takes
Is my responsibility

Sarah
I promise I had no idea what you were really going through
So please forgive me
Please don't hate me
It feels so wrong to experience happiness
When you're not standing right beside me
I'm up on this stage tonight
Missing you pretty badly
Because in 5 days from now
You would have turned 23
I think you would've liked being up on this stage too
An artistic theater girl like you reading poetry
The thought makes me smile
Even though I really want to cry
Because after 6 1/2 years
The truth is
I can't even remember what my own sister sounded like
I wonder
When I step up to this mic
Do my desperate cries rise up to Heaven
And land on your ears
I know everyone's probably sick of me bringing you up
But I really don't care
I refuse to pretend as if you were never there
So until the day comes
When my bleeding heart runs dry
I will keep on writing
Rhymes about you
Until everyone else around me feels like you were their sister too

amorphous.
Deane Aldric, Florence

sometimes i feel like an amorphous mass
like my body has no shape, no solid form
i simply exist, in a shape unknown to me
who can tell what i actually look like?
who can see the person i am underneath
these many layers of added protection?
hello? can anyone see me?

i sometimes feel trapped in my own body
it weighs me down, limits me in ways i can't quite explain
i often wish i could escape
the prison of my own flesh
and be the person i know i truly am
hello? can anyone hear me?

i sometimes feel an itch in my bones
as if they want to escape from under my skin
leaping out and feeling the sun for the first time
i often get the urge to help it escape
to allow it an exit by way of a blade
so i may be free for once in my life
hello? can anyone help me?

i sometimes feel as though i wear a mask
smiling for all to see, stitched of flesh and sinew
fixed into a single position
never allowing me to show what i feel
i often wonder what would happen
if i ripped it off
exposing my true colors
allowing myself to be authentic
unapologetic
no longer amorphous
simply me
hello? can anyone see me?

we always want bones
Avery Volk, Phoenix

was there ever enough of me in your marrow/sucking out your pale sustenance/as winter's hollow thickness turns dark and/looks/once more at its own sickness/everything is frozen over/can we go home yet/the laughter of children sets my teeth on edge and makes me want to go deaf/I can't see anything anymore through the fog/except/I can still hear you calling me at all hours of the night/now finally I've given you a place to rest your bones and I wonder/if/all the pain and sickness you carried in your earthly body/has faded out/and been carried away with the/bitter cold and ash/the taste of ash in my mouth is too fitting/how I wanted to put it in yours/instead/I watch the clock and/time/loses all meaning/instead/I just watch the memories

– we always want bones

I was born in the middle of a house fire.

Rowe Alán Casales, Phoenix

I was born in the middle of a house fire.
The youngest of four siblings in a failing marriage;
I was that baby that was meant to resuscitate the body of a relationship that was 9 years
dead on arrival,
But goddamnit, my father was determined to save it, even if that meant burning us all to
ash together in the end.

Because of this,
I grew up thinking that love wasn't real if you didn't get a little burned in the process
so please believe it when I say that I have only ever learned to love someone
the "wrong way."

how do you recognize the warning signs when the smoke in a burning building has
always smelled just like home?

My father's love was an oil-slicked bird cage.
When my mother was finally free of it,
She spent years running away from relationships,
As if, if she were to settle down, even for a moment,
She would once again wake up
burning behind those bars.

I am convinced
That there are still parts of her that never really made it out of those flames.

She was replaced by a dragon.
"Hell hath no fury like a woman scorned"
but I think she just didn't want to be hurt like that again so
My mother cooked innocent men up for pleasure,
Hung them out to dry,
And usually got rid of them whenever things got too messy.

As I got older,
I fell in love with people who were just like my parents.
Hurt women whose love branded you like a hot iron.
Problematic men with pyromaniac tendencies.

People who didn't come with fire alarms,
that I could

deep dive into the flames for and pull them out of their very own wreckage,

But no one can really prepare you for how painful it feels to hold onto a burning body or how quickly fire catches.

Maybe that's why those relationships always failed,
And why I'd spent most of my time looking for an exit sign.

Featured Poet:

VALENCE

Tyler "VALENCE" Sirvinskas is an American citizen, maternally of the African Diaspora, paternally Polish & Lithuanian. He was born & raised in the south suburbs of Chicago, and grew up in Arizona. His maternal grandmother taught him to sew by hand when he was fourteen years old. He discovered the Flagstaff, AZ poetry slam in 2009 and has been performing ever since.

His artistic rapsheet includes:
- 2010 ‹Flagslam›, 2011 ‹Sedona›, & 2012 ‹Sedona› National Poetry Slam team member
- 2011 Sedona Poetry Slam Grand Slam Champion
- 2024 Chicharra Poetry Slam Festival ‹team Route 666›
- Founder & Creative Director of ATELIER VALENCE, which produces apparel & accessories

2 A.M.

the 2 A.M. is so quiet
I can hear the cigarette burning.
I am reaching up, pretending to hold the moon
between my fingers– feeling small.
I'm convinced that some tomorrows reach us
too weary to lift our spirits.
something is lost as the sun rises over the Atlantic
and my midday smoke break feels like the leftovers
of Sydney or Cairo.
on the bad days,
wilting hourglass and claustrophobia.
I'm learning the word heavy all over again.
today is London's hand-me-down
with all the fog intact.
I am thankful the laughs are cheap,
though sometimes few and far between-
on the bad days, I look you in the eyes and wonder
if there's room enough for me in your tomorrow.
so stay close.
I already miss the you
that isn't shaky with anticipation
over the separation anxiety that will follow this-
and there are seven billion people
that I don't want to wade through
so I can breathe you in.
and that loneliness is a feeling
we will allow to compromise us,
but when life disentwines us
it is easier to joke that our wanderlust
would have had its way with us sooner or later-
it is easier to joke than to admit
that our bodies do not ask permission to heal,
and our hearts will again learn to open
like perennials after the frost.

I won't say nothing's wrong.

and maybe you don't believe in God
but I know you believe in the ghosts-
and I've seen you float before.
seen you try shouldering the world with a notebook.
young Atlas, do you tremble?
let the wind take you, then.
it's funny isn't it?
it seems like just yesterday this house was new.
I used to think lives could fit neatly in boxes
but no matter the size of the home
or the price of the coffin it just isn't so.
we fit together awkwardly in a jostle tectonic.
we collide seismically then simply drift apart.
we leave for strange places, become strangers,
and as fast as we move it happens all too quickly-
and we're so tired, aren't we?
so show me where it hurts.
I'll show you mine if you show me yours-
these days it feels like some of us
will do anything to distract from the sight
of year after year just flying by in the mirror
but I want more.
how many times have we stopped
to look back in awe as the heart swells immense?
airports, funeral processions,
the nest, finally quiet-
how swift our departures.
but what is old? what is old
when the dream comes fresh?
put your hand on your heart
and tell me who's in there.
a compass if I've ever seen one. a pledge-
that finding our way
doesn't always make sense
but stay close together and I promise
God does the rest

Bus Rides & Bird Wings

I am waiting for the bus
when a bird emerges from behind a trash can.
it is hurt, hopping on one leg,
and I know it is hungry.
I open a packet of crackers and set one on the ground.
as the bird cautiously pecks away,
the woman beside me
guesses at the extent of the injury.
she suggests that with wings intact
the bird may yet live.
a man in a wheelchair reminds her
that a broken leg
means a crash landing every time.
the other woman on the bench
is wrapped up in her own distress,
trying not to cry.
my phone rings.
failed driving record check,
rescinded offer of employment.
the bus ride is long
and I talk to God for most of it.
at my stop, I see the road over
is closed off with caution tape.
among the emergency vehicles
I see the telling red of a coroner's van;
my god, the suffering.
the struggle.
the ties that bind.
a marriage of delusion and folly–
my heart plays the wedding march.
honest beginnings.
bitter ends.
I reminisce often.
to absent friends-
I've left a glass on the table for you.

I say your names out loud–
it is the sound of a deep root
being torn loose.
how many nights have you been closer
than these beating hearts I pass by
in crowd after crowd?

I leave a candle in my windowsill
for something that will never return.

tonight,
I will walk my dead
from the boneyard to the shore.
dozens of gondolas will float in wait,
shrouded ferrymen aboard
idly stirring their paddles in slow circles.
one by one, their lanterns begin to glow.
I pray quietly as my dearly departed begin to go,
taking their seats and ebbing slowly out to sea.
they are survived by me,
and this is what that means.
at dawn, I dark my candle
as gently as you would stroke the fur
of a wounded thing.
we will say good morning-
and I will tell you
I've had such strange dreams.
I have braids of sweet grass for your hearth
and cautious tidings for the season ahead.
for these streets, like a river,
leave the husks of men washed up on its banks.
cross with the light,
for you ford what is precious
through perilous straits.
I will keep an eye and a prayer out for you–
I hope you'll do the same.

Ones & Twos

one. for the quiet ones.
who know what it is to be invisible.
in the back of the room listening close
but afraid to be seen
their eyes lit up with words and sparks
dancing the way they've always wished to.
and it's been so long since I went dancing.
do you lay awake at night like I do?
my heart does this impression of a revolving door—
forgets what it is sometimes.
know I think the world of you.
have heard you speak and swore it came
from a place too vast to be within you.
and I know we have walked through hell.
for these days it seems we are all but caught
in the passing breeze
our tongues, hauling up an anchor,
struggling with the words accordingly, they say
how dare a dream ask mercy
in this world of sleepless nights
and sinking Venice
where the shoreline erases footprints
with slow and utter indifference.
I have seen the love
that turns back into shadow and gold at dawn–
and the moon is out early.
you should say a prayer, for this night may be long
and we all have something to lose
but good days are coming.
harvest. autumn approaches
as the season of temperance and determination
we will greet the winter ready
for the long nights to soften us
bless the kingless english of your silver tongue,
and continue to swing it
as though it could not break your teeth.

two. dear Persephone—
do you remember the burning skyline
and my head in your lap?
I was hiding even then,
learning every fix for a racing heartbeat.
we were windswept
and so sure that what we touched
would turn to gold; the breeze
would taste our laughter
and sing for us.
wandering but never lost,
nothing but sparks between us and the city so alive—
we were living then.
covering our fright with butterflies
I have since pinned to wood
and framed under glass.

we know there is no going back and you
are learning every inch of his heart
in your kitchen full of magic.
and I
have learned all there is to know
about building up walls.
I've gone silver, gone cold, just gone—
you still light up
e v e r y thing
and I still fold my wings
to hide that I've fallen, but
you remember
how my feathers match your foxbones...
don't you?

Rainstorm

Social Anxiety
Ej, Phoenix

I hope you don't think I'm weird.

I stare not out of obsession—
perhaps I'm hyper-fixated.
Studying every detail of you,
mapping the contours of your presence.

I wish you could read my mind,
come speak to me.
But once you're out of sight,
I'll move on.

I imagine—
every possible scenario,
every choice of words,
every fleeting thought,
every outcome.
I freeze.

The fear of judgment.
The fear of being ridiculed.
The fear of never measuring up.
They paralyze me.

To word-vomit
or
not to word-vomit—
that is the question.
Skip the small talk.
Lay everything bare.
But that's not okay.

I really hope you don't think I'm weird.

One Day
Kassie R. Black, Phoenix

In the hushed cocoon of the night,
beneath the weight of a restless sky,
a mother leans close, whispers softly,
the rhythm of her heart, a lullaby.
"Listen, my love, to the world outside,
where the thunder roars and shadows collide.
But one day, oh child, when the darkness gives way,
the bombs will fall silent, and peace will stay."
She brushes the hair from his forehead,
each stroke a promise, a gentle thread,
binding their hopes to the stars above,
where dreams still flourish, where fear cannot shove.
"In the gardens of morning, with dew on the grass,
we'll dance in the sunlight, let the past pass.
And flowers will bloom in colors so bright,
a tapestry woven with joy and with light."
His eyes, wide and shining, search her face,
seeking the warmth of that promised place.
"Will there be laughter? Will there be friends?"
"In the embrace of love, that never ends?"
So they shelter together, her arms a shield,
as echoes of sorrow through the night yield.
"Hold tight to my words, let them nest in your heart,
for love is the force that can heal and restart."
"Though the world may tremble and darkness may creep,
I'll guard you with dreams, and we'll both dare to sleep.
For one day, my darling, the bombs will subside,
and we'll walk hand in hand, with hope as our guide."

Ode To the Woo Woo Woo
Joey Scribbles, Phoenix

The everyday man's ellipses
Used to shorten a story from
Being longer than a George RR Martin novel
To being flash fiction, to get to the point.
Used by cousins to boast and skip
Over details they want to evade
To get to the crux of the story
That they can boast about
At family reunions.

Uncles and fathers give vague details and pieces
Of their past sins for their successors
To use as a life lesson
Or to glorify and boast about whatever it is they did.

Practiced by many to be speedy storytellers
Who tell tales to a hasty audience
Whose time is held precious to him or her
Not wanting one wasted minute to occur.

You are a linguistic treasure to remind us
Of how much brevity is needed.
Skim off the fact of what is not needed
And only include what is vital.

You are an appropriate tool for the times
In a world where attention is as long
As a man's eyelashes.
A story can only run on a long line
Until it burns out.
It has to hit the road and rubber
Needs to get to the burning point
By the time a person says …
So what happened was
And he better get it running.
Otherwise, the road to ears will soon
Become a dead end.

"Eye am"
Jay Gó, Phoenix

Who am I?
I'm first generation
with the realization
No soy de aquí ni de allí
neither I'm from here nor from there.

Spanish was my foundation.
And I thought English
would be my salvation
and validation.

Grasping at words.
To express my frustration.
To the alienation.
And discrimination
Of being first generation.

So I diligently learned pronunciation.
Like an incantation.
Pizzza.
No, it's Pete—za
Horror-ible.
No, it's whore—able

And when I write in my speaking voice.
I'm quickly quieted by the gatekeepers.
Into subjugation.

A lifetime of correction.
Lost in translation.
Existing in a world of condemnation
And segmentation.

My actions and intentions unseen
instead tongue tied,
I'm the center of attention
For the wrong intention.

So I laugh it off,

To appease
Your inconsideration,
To the fact, I'm not from here nor there,
Cause I'm first generation.

When I'm there
I'm out with pride
And veneration
Because I'm their propagation.

Who am I?
I arrived with inspiration
in 1982
A child of immigrants
Demanding my birth right and repatriation
Born in a city of Angels.
without a name.
God's purpose ingrained.

In the humble office of Dr. Finesse.
I was born like a king.
So I can't complain
Asked to name me Jeannette,
God is gracious.
And my güerita named me Lupita
blessed me,
With a divine name.

My mother married young.
And in desperation
Hustled from the early morn to the late eve.
A green eyed mamacita
Puro Navojoa, Sonora.
Danced like a firefly,
Towards her expatriation
Waiting for gasoline,
To ignite her unrealized dreams.
Dancing her way to LA.
Towards the fruition of her aspirations.

Who am I?
I am my mother, and she Is I.
She's the hustle to my flow.
And the grind to my hustle.
Horizons full of exploration.

Cruising to the funky beat.

2018, was her expiration.
Towards her destination
I couldn't go.
Yet somehow,
I perished then too.
reincarnated with a different soul.

Exited my chrysalis painfully.
out came an artist, a poet,
an activist of love.
And everything in between.

A child of God.
Reborn from the ashes.
in the city of the Sun,
Like a Phoenix.
IS WHO I am…

But not less than first generation.

My Body
Hallie Pahl, Scottsdale

As I tie this triangle bikini around my neck, I realize it was never this easy to

simply exist with my body.

Instead I've had the same thought play on loop

since I discovered hating my body at age 10 …

It repeats

When I am skinny, then I will be happy.

I believed I only had the permission to exist

once I took up less space.

Scrutinized stomach for not flattening like a wooden plank,

Pinched the fat around my body

Wishing I could simply cut it off with scissors.

Sand down bumpy patches of cellulite on my thighs,

And erase stretch marks evident on my hips.

Every moment alone with my reflection in the mirror

I wasn't actually looking at myself

I was thoroughly inspecting myself for flaw

Turning side to side to criticize every angle

Soon my body dysmorphia graduated to eating disorders

Acquainting myself with Ana and Mia

Becoming too familiar with calorie counting and my gag reflex

Motivated by the distant happiness

I would finally gain if I had a smaller body

That same broken record spun me to breakdowns insisting

When I am Skinny

Then I will be allowed to be happy

When I take up less space

Then I will be allowed to exist

But I am proud to do a lot more than just existing

No my body was not built to be skinny

My body is shaped in the likeness of a timeless hourglass

My body winds with curves and cascades

My body has twists and turns that you can get lost in

As I wear this triangle bikini

I realized how grateful I am to be released

From this hell of looking at my body with disappointment

Instead of gratitude

waiting for rain
Skyelyn Riggs-Davis, Mesa

i often speak my truth without considering the weight of it

without remembering that it takes

a slow coax

a simmering roast

a trail of cheerios

for us to accept a new reality.

how do you boil a frog?

by slowly turning up the heat

with change that doesn't seem like change until you're dead and cooked.

my truths have never come to me in epiphany

yet i still meet people with a clap of thunder

when there's barely a cloud in the sky,

forgetting that for most

seeing is believing-

if there's no clouds

how could you believe in the thunder?

if the sky is clear

how could you believe a storm is on the horizon?

i'm chicken little

i'm boy who cried wolf

i'm tree fallen in the forest

i'm a case study in einstein's relativity

screaming my truth

doing my absolute best

to attest to what i see

moving at a different velocity-

nothing looks as it once did

when i used to swim with the school of fish

does a beached whale also die of loneliness?

i wish things were different

but what i've learned is this:

if you scream your truth,

no one's going to believe you.

but if you whisper it delicately,

let it simmer-

they just might.

49/50
Raad Syed, Phoenix

I am a product of the Arizona education system! When ranking the states in terms of quality of education, we were ranked 49 out of 50 – which is perfect because I always feel like the 2nd dumbest person in a room.

This one's for Hamilton High School home of the Hamilton Huskies.

This one's for Social Studies class where we did a "holocaust simulation" the students did wall-sits outside for 30 minutes, the teacher reached into one of the students backpack, took out her lunchbox, started eating her sandwich looked at us and said "the Nazis did way worse."
Remember when they took our sandwiches during the holocaust?

This one's for the U.S history class, where our teacher's favorite president was Andrew Jackson.
Your favorite president doesn't have to be one that killed over 10,000 native Americans. You can just say Lincoln.

This one's for the Hamilton Hotties club, an invite only group for the hottest highschool girls?
This one's for Taylor – wondering why her friend Sarah got an invite and she didn't. You should have followed the two simple rules Step 1. Make sure your skin is pale Step 2. Double check the number on the scale. A Hamilton Husky should never be husky. It didn't matter what you were like or what you liked but how many likes and how you liked. You know, like talking like something like this as if the filler polluting each of your sentences could be used to fill the empty husk that is your personality.

This one's for the seniors on the Hamilton Football team, tried with 9 counts of sexual assault for what they did to the 15 year old freshmen on the team. You spent your entire senior year in jail…And STILL peaked in High School.

This one's for the faculty who misheard teaching for tyranny, for the former friends who never grew up because they were too scared they wouldn't be able to.

What I learned in highschool still has me feeling stupid. I was on a date and the woman reached into my basket of fries, stealing my food, so I looked her in the eye and I said "You know my teacher taught me that this type of behavior led to the death of 6 million Jews"

This one's for the teacher…Who taught me that my words could have an impact on people. For the teacher who stayed after school so my friend and I could host the competitive Pokemon club– even though we only had 3 members (including us). For the teacher who did not mistake my lost voice for a lost cause.

There's a reason Arizona wasn't ranked last. 50/50. It's thanks to you…
That we're not fucking Arkansas.

Collaborators
Este Amané Williams, Phoenix

They lied on our ancestors, they lied on us, they lie to our children.
They instruct us to earn our keep. Keep watch over what is yours, even though nothing
(that they find worth in) is yours.
We are sold the indentured life, with hidden fees, packaged in the thin veil of the promise
and pride of freedom.

You never consented. And your vote is not your consent, but nightstick-obedience.
Sometimes the only choice you have is to die. Sometimes your only choice is to hope that
someone's descendants, if not yours, will be birthed into—birth themselves into—a
different world. Where sharecrop contracts of consent are not valued by rotting
constitutions.
We pray for this. Pray it into being.
We are being. Still, somehow, as we are used and destroyed.
So keep on.

Create stories of comfort and legend that will be lost to everyone but those who are
listening.
With patience, teach your young to listen,
and implore your elders to follow the dreams of the young.
They have been here before, too.

Look back, and look around, and look forward, and be it ruins or rich soil,
plant your feet on solid ground.
Soothe your soles in calm lapping waters.
Whisper until it is our time to stomp.

We build tsunami waves with the movements of our lips, until we create the shaking.
Until the lies crumble and collapse
under the weight of their own poison;
which strengthened us,
even as it halved our flock.

Move our hands together and pull brothers caught under from the rubble.
Drink in the thick air.
Now we are liberated.

Now, we can create anything. Lies will destroy us no more.
Where they collude, we collaborate.

So lay down and rest.

The work is done.

The working has just begun.

Featured Poet:

Cag Loveless

Cag Loveless recently moved to Mesa, Arizona from northeast Indiana. They graduated from Purdue University Fort Wayne at the beginning of this year with a B.A. in theatre, and a minor in creative writing. They were published in the PFW student magazine "Confluence" in the spring of 2023. Cag works closely with tying in elements of theatre and the stage with writing. They tackle themes of identity, survival, and family in both plays and poems. They taught a masterclass at Ball State University in the fall of 2023 about connecting poetry and voice in performance, using their poem "you bring out the non-binary in me." Cag wrote a play called "The Paradox of Choice" for a class, which was put on as a staged reading. They used elements of poetic rhythm and Shakespearean iambic pentameter to develop characters, and presented their research on that in the 2024 Research and Creative Endeavors Symposium at Purdue Fort Wayne. Aside from writing, Cag is an avid performer and worked as a contracted actor with various theatre companies across Indiana. Cag studied poetry under the poet laureate of Indiana, Curtis Crisler, and would like to thank him for the endless support and "Bam!"s.

I WILL SING FOR YOU

quite often, when i would see my father, i would sing for him.
i would sing with my eyes closed, and i would close my eyes
so i didn't have to bear witness to the tears streaming down his goatee.
i would sing for him when he was away, too, which was more often than not.
i would sing for him through glass windows, into landline telephones.
most of the time he could not even hear me, and *i wish i could be silent more.*

he's not special though, i sing for anything that fills me with a pit
and makes me feel like i am going to pop.
i sing for him the day after he tells me he wants to be there to walk me down the aisle,
and i sing the song that says he's not.
i sing for him the day he tells me the phone goes both ways,
and i sing the song that blocks his number and makes that untrue.

i'm learning so many different ways to be quiet.
but i still sing for him now, even after he's nothing but a box full of ash.

DEAR GOD: IT'S ME AGAIN. SORRY, I KNOW YOU DON'T LIKE ME.

mom took us to church for three weeks in a row
"it would be good for you," my aunt said.
they thought they could find salvation for me.
i was told *god's plan*
included the time my father left me in a cold car overnight
and when my uncle put his hands on me in places he shouldn't.
i didn't understand why *god's plan*
would make *'lil nine year old me*
think i was a burden on god himself.

**

crossroads church in "crossroads, indiana"
said i was going to hell if i didn't talk to god.
but i didn't like closing my eyes and listening to the sound of only my own breath for that long.
in. out. in. out. "god, why can't i hear you like everyone else,
don't you wanna talk to me?"
the chapel looked like a warehouse, with tall, clean white walls.
dirtied only by the giant brown cross.
they kept the worship drummer in a clear box
"do they let him out after church?"

**

my clothes weren't as nice as the other kids'
i wore the same lavender easter sunday dress from walmart
all three sundays in a row.
my friend, the daughter of the pastor,
said he was wondering when we would "return and walk with god again."
we haven't talked since then, and that was fourth grade
and i'm twenty-one now and *still can't hear god.*
i've never yelled for him–i don't scream, i don't cry–only whisper.
maybe i should be louder for my own salvation.
(or maybe god should've listened harder.)

I AM A PAPER BAG

i am a paper bag from the chinese takeout restaurant down the street.
the food was ordered and eaten three weeks ago,
but i am still sitting, crumpled on the floor.
a brown paper bag, with a grease stain on the side.
the trash gets taken out, but i just sit here.
i'm not trash enough to be thrown out.
and i'm not useful enough to be valued.
i wish i could tear myself up,
so that someone would notice the mess
and discard me, properly.
my foot is the corner of the bag,
stuck underneath the creaky recliner,
slowly being torn everytime the chair rocks.
the pain is dull, tormenting.
i will it to go away but the chair keeps on.
they still don't take me out to the dumpster,
where i belong.
the cats have taken a liking to me.
they purr and headbutt the opening,
trying to get me to open up
so they can reach my heart in the deep cavern of paper.
i am a toy to the felines.
one tabby, and the other black.
their claws tear the folds of my flimsy structure,
but the love is worth the pain.
at least someone sees me as more than a paper bag,
ready for the trash.

The River
Kaden Presley, Gilbert

Water-
canvas for existence
flowing in veins
a cosmic earth we create
subject to mercurial reality
we flow
and we flow
turning gears in our brains
to set a new course
beating
and onward

Guided by our hearts
we are mad
we are born
we are foaming
and frothing
at the mouth of the river
where we make our surrender

The great holy river
is never
never
ending

End. End. End.
After End.